Five Minutes to Mindfulness

How's the Weather Today?

My Feelings Forecast

Written & Illustrated by

Ashleigh Stewart
&
Robbie & Tiffany Stewart-Ghabi

How's the Weather Today?

Copyright © 2017 LittleLightHouse Publishing

All rights reserved.
No part of this book may be reproduced in any written, electronic, recording, or photocopying form without written permission of the publisher.

Written & Illustrated by
Ashleigh Stewart
&
Robbie & Tiffany Stewart-Ghabi

ISBN: 978-09953090-3-6

Printed in Canada

A book about feelings for children aged 4-8

My Feelings Forecast

"*Emotion is the language of the Spirit*"
- Ashleigh Stewart

This Book Belongs To

_____

How's the Weather Today?
My Feelings Forecast
Review

Pick a day, any day and we talk about the weather. It's how we greet each other; a grumble about the rain or a cheery quip about a perfectly sunny day. What better way to introduce the idea of feelings, emotions, and self-regulation than by using a subject with which children are already familiar. Ashleigh Stewart and her children, Robbie and Tiffany, have written and illustrated a wonderfully easy introduction to thinking and talking about feelings.

As a teacher, I can dive right into self-regulation without pre-teaching new vocabulary and abstract concepts. Children understand the weather and how the weather makes them feel. How's the Weather Today? My Feelings Forecast is an immediately useable source for parents and teachers who want to give children a way to explain their feelings and begin to manage them. It is simple enough for pre-schoolers and complex enough for pre-teens. I can see teachers using it as part of their daily calendar routine or as an opening conversation to lessons on self-awareness, self-regulation, puberty, and inter-personal relationships.

Graeme Cotton
Teacher, Vancouver School Board
BA, PDPP, MA
Governor General's Award for Excellence in Teaching 2013

"How's the Weather Today?" is a wonderful book for children to learn how to understand their feelings better. The "nature" of feelings is best described in comparison to the weather. This is a brilliant analogy in that kids can understand how feelings, like the weather, comes and goes and feelings are natural and "okay" to express just like how the weather manifests itself in different ways. This book is a very helpful resource for parents and teachers to support them in helping children be mindful of what feelings are all about.

Kaye Liao Banez
Author of "See Yah in the Morning! A bedtime story" children's book. She is also a mom of two children and a fierce advocate for autism awareness and inclusion.

bammstellacreations.com

A Message for Grown-Ups

We wrote this book for children. The intention is to help educate them about the daily awareness of their feelings in a way that is light-hearted and fun. I chose the weather theme because it provides a useful metaphor for describing emotion, and is something that children can easily identify with. The other interesting thing about the weather is that it is something that most of us pay attention to, in fact we check it daily. The weather is important. We use it as a guide to planning many parts of our day, for example, our activity schedule, our clothing, and even what mode of transportation we take. The weather is a fundamental part of how we choose to live out our lives each day.

I believe it is just as important for children, and adults too, to learn to check in with how they are feeling each day. Awareness of your feelings is a first step toward emotional and mental well-being. How you feel is also an important indicator of how the day will go, as many of us allow our feelings to dictate the outcome of our experiences each day. We often think 'I feel sad, therefore the day will be bad', or 'I feel happy, therefore, the day will be good'. Although our emotions are an important indicator of how we will experience our life, it need not be in complete control of it. In fact we can learn to be in charge of our own emotions, and how we allow them to affect us. This is what this book is about.

Mindfulness is at the root of the majority of all the work I do with children, and with adults too. When you are living mindfully, you are rooted in the present moment. That means that you are aware of what is going on now, no matter whether it feels good or bad. When you are aware of your feelings and how they are affecting you, they can then be altered intentionally. This moment of mindful emotional awareness is where healing and personal growth begins.

The use of repetitive language in this book in intended to speak to the subconscious mind. It is through repetition that our brains are wired, and learning occurs. As human beings, we are creatures of habit and all behavior and belief begins, and can also end with continuous repetition of a pattern of words, thoughts and feelings.

Most of the images in the book are set in the same landscape. This feature is also intended to enhance the idea of repetition and create a sense of familiarity. However, the same landscape is shown in different ways according to the weather. This illustrates the idea that we can be in the same place or 'experience', yet feel it differently depending on our mood and emotions.

It is important use the words "I feel" when describing emotions to children, as oppose to the words "I am". This is because it is important that children learn their emotions are something that they experience, and that they can be fleeting. Emotions are not something that defines who they are, and can be changed at any time with deliberate intention.

Points to consider when reading this book to your child:

- Children, and who they are should not be defined or labeled according to their emotions, their emotions are something that they experience.

- Emotions are mainly influenced by external circumstances, therefore can be altered when a circumstance, or situation in their environment is changed.

- Weather is good example of an external experience which can influence the way you feel.

- Simplicity is key with children. When reading this book with them, look for simple language of which they can relate to with as feeling, such as bright, cheerful, heavy, or busy for example.

My own children helped me to write this book. In essence, this book was written by children, for children. I hope you will find it to be a useful and fun tool which will help you get off on the right foot when it comes to helping your child develop a healthy sense of self awareness and emotional intelligence from an early age. I hope that both you and your child, or children enjoy reading this book.

Ashleigh

How's the weather today?
It looks like the sun is coming out. Everything feels warm and bright. I can hear the birds singing!

Today I feel happy!

What are some words that describe how you feel when you feel happy?

_____

_____

_____

My Feelings Forecast

How's the weather today?
It looks like it is raining. Everything feels cold and wet. The sky is heavy with clouds. It seems like they are crying.

Today I feel sad.

What are some words that describe how you feel when you are sad?

_____

_____

_____

My Feelings Forecast

How's the Weather Today?

How's the weather today?
It looks like it is raining, yet the sun is shining too. Oh look there's a rainbow! Oh dear, today I feel a little unsure.

What are some words that describe how you feel when you feel unsure?

_____

_____

_____

My Feelings Forecast

How's the weather today?

It looks like a stormy day. The sky looks very dark. I can hear loud noises like rumbling and crackling. There are bright flashes of lightning too. The clouds look really mad! Today I feel angry.

What are some words that describe how you feel when you feel angry?

_____

_____

_____

My Feelings Forecast

How's the weather today? It looks so windy today. The clouds seem to have a lot of energy. They are blowing things about. Everything is moving so fast! I feel very anxious!

What are some words that describe how you feel when you feel anxious?

_____

_____

_____

My Feelings Forecast

How's the weather today?

It looks like a snowy day! Snow is falling from the clouds oh so gently. The clouds look like marshmallows! So does the snow on the ground! Everything seems so still.

I feel so calm!

What are some words that describe how you feel when you feel calm?

My Feelings Forecast

The day is now coming to an end, and night is falling. The clouds have lifted high. The sky is getting dark, but the moon is shining bright. So are the stars.

Look at how they twinkle!

Everything is so quiet. I feel very tired now.

It is time to go to sleep.

Goodnight. Zzzzzzz

My Feelings Forecast

Good morning!

It's a new day. The sun is coming up in the sky. I can hear the birds singing. It feels like a great day today, and no matter the weather, be it wind, rain or storm, any day is a great day to be happy!

THE END

My Feelings Forecast

ABOUT THE AUTHORS

Dr. Ashleigh Stewart Msc.D.

Author, Metaphysical Counselor, Therapeutic Yoga Instructor & Holistic Health Expert

Ashleigh's studies started in the field of Psychology however; the scientific approach to the study of the mind did not satisfy her interest in the mind/body connection, and so she switched her focus toward to the holistic approach of spiritual psychotherapy, holistic biochemistry and metaphysical science.

Ashleigh eventually was awarded her doctorate in metaphysical counseling, where her concentration was therapeutic yoga, during which she studied the effects of stimulant drugs upon children, and therapeutic yoga as a natural approach to treating children diagnosed with ADHD.

Ashleigh is a certified yoga instructor of the 'Bali Method of Therapeutic Yoga' and has been teaching yoga and meditation to children and adults for over 10 years.

Ashleigh's experience with children extends beyond teaching yoga. She a family childcare in her home during the years she stayed at home after having had her own two children. She is a certified in Infant & Child First Aid & CPR certified in Fundamentals of Family Childcare, Introduction to Science & Physical Education for Family Child Care and Nutrition Basics for Children. As a hobby, she teaches a community program in the local after school club where she bakes with the children.

Visit the author's websites at www.fiveminutestominmdfulness.com and www.littlelighthouseyoga.com to obtain 25% off the purchase of an online program, or product with coupon code 5MINSTOMINDFULNESSKIDS

My Feelings Forecast

Robbie Stewart-Ghabi

Robbie Stewart-Ghabi, co-author of 'My Feeling's Forecast' is Ashleigh's ten year old son. Robbie is experienced in the practice of yoga and mindfulness, and the Zones of Regulation, a curriculum designed to promote self-regulation and emotional awareness. His knowledge of the curriculum is what inspired him to help his mother Ashleigh write, and illustrate 'My Feelings Forecast'. Robbie is a very kind hearted boy, who enjoys helping and supporting younger children in the Big Buddies program at his school. His hobbies are soccer, reading and watching cooking shows.

Tiffany Stewart-Ghabi

Tiffany Stewart-Ghabi, co-author of 'My Feeling's Forecast' is Ashleigh's nine year old daughter. During grade two, Tiffany attended a ten week program at a social and emotional learning center. Her knowledge of social and emotional learning inspired her to help her mother Ashleigh write and illustrate the book 'My Feelings Forecast'. Tiffany has practiced yoga and mindfulness, and art as extra curriculum activities since kindergarten. Like her brother Robbie, she is also enjoying being a part of the Big Buddies program at school, by supporting and being an example to younger children. Tiffany's hobbies are baking, soccer and riding her scooter. She also loves to watch cooking shows.

www.ingramcontent.com/pod-product-compliance
Lightning Source LLC
Chambersburg PA
CBHW040023050426
42452CB00002B/106